CW00524095

Wirksworth
in old picture postcards

Tony Holmes

European Library ZALTBOMMEL/THE NETHERLANDS

GB ISBN 90 288 2200 3

© 2000 European Library – Zaltbommel/The Netherlands

European Library

post office box 49

NL – 5300 AA Zaltbommel/The Netherlands

telephone: 0031 418 513144

fax: 0031 418 515515

e-mail:publisher@eurobib.nl

Introduction

The pace of change in Wirksworth has not been constant but continued at an ever-increasing rate in the last hundred years. Although Wirksworth has been described as a sleepy town at the head of the Ecclesbourne valley, it has not escaped the march of time. People's way of life and earning a living have completely changed.

The biggest change in the last hundred years has been in the mode of transport. At the end of the Victorian age, the main means of transport would be the railways and the horse and cart or carriage. In Wirksworth, there would be the rush of farmers with carts full of milk churns, to catch the early morning train to transport the milk to the cities. After the First World War, horse transport gave way to the automobile with lorries and buses opening up speedier ways of getting to new and old destinations. After the Second World War, the convenience of lorries ousted the railways in the delivery business and buses declined with the advent of cheap cars. Today the early morning rush is people in cars rushing out of Wirksworth to work in the neighbouring towns and cities. The streets have become cluttered with cars.

In the early 1900's, the town was self-contained in providing employment for most of its inhabitants in the quarries, farms, tape mills, shops and other necessary services. At the end of the Victorian period the town was prosperous. At daylight there would be the clatter of the quarrymen's boots on the stone setts on their way to the quarries. The smoke from the numerous limekilns would hang over the town like a large cloud. The quarries would echo to the sounds of many hammers breaking the limestone into the correct shapes. The women would be off to the mills and their noisy weaving looms to make miles and miles of red tape.

The advent of electricity in the town in the thirties saw steam and gas engines gradually replaced with electric motors, which were more efficient. The 1930s recession was to bring considerable hardship to the quarry men and others. The building of Harrison Drive in 1938 eased traffic problems but let the north wind into the town. The quarries were mechanized in the mid-1950s, making nearly 500 men, who had to seek work elsewhere, redundant. The town never recovered from this and although a number of small industries exist around the town today, 80 percent of the workforce commute to other areas to work. Now the quarries are closed, the dust has settled and Wirksworth is a pleasant place to live.

From the 1930s through to the 1960s, the fabric of the town gradually declined and many old buildings were demolished, as there was no money for repairs. After the Second World War, the standard of housing was very poor and the Derby Road council estates were built to ease this situation. Private house building has continued to the south-west of the town. The fabric of the old town was extensively overhauled in 1980 resulting in the presentation of the Europa Nostra Award for architectural conservation in 1983.

In the early 1900s, the shops in the town catered for the tastes and necessities of residents and industry. This pattern of shopping continued until the 1950s, when modern supermarkets started to appear. Gradually the number of shops declined, as people shopped the modern way. Little shops in North End, Bolehill, Gorsey Bank and Millers Green have disappeared. Institutions like Marsdens, where you could buy anything in hardware, electrical or agricultural, have gone. Today, we can only buy a small selection of goods in the town and the number of shops has declined with the change in shopping habits.

The pictures in the book have been arranged so that a circular walk around the old town can be taken to view what is left of our heritage. I wonder what Wirksworth will look like at the end of 2100?

Special thanks to all the people who over the years have passed on bits of information and lent pictures to build this glimpse of twentieth century Wirksworth.

1 One of the first sights to greet the visitor is that of Haarlem Mill and Adam Bede Cottage. The mill buildings on the left were erected in three stages in 1885. The small buildings to the left and right of the mill house have disappeared. In the early 1800s, Adam Bede Cottage was the home of Samuel and Elizabeth Evans, who were immortalized as the hero and heroine in the book 'Adam Bede' by George Eliot (niece of Elizabeth Evans). The mill is now home to a water treatment company.

Adam Bede's Cottage and Haarlem Mills, Wirksworth.

2   To the north of the mill was a millpond, which stretched along Derby Road and halfway along Cinder Lane. A brook coming from Sprink Wood fed the millpond. By 1950 the millpond was silted up and has been filled in. A modern factory extension now stands on part of the site. The lower gritstone part of the building was the original mill built by Arkwright after 1777, and was built on the site of a much older mill that was used for fulling and lead smelting. Arkwright purchased a steam engine around 1800 to pump water from the tailrace to the millpond. The mill and millpond were mentioned in George Eliot's novel 'Adam Bede'.

3   Around 1950, Adam Bede Cottage was one of the petrol stations in the town and sold Cleveland petrol. The required amount of petrol was hand-pumped into a glass vessel near the top of the pump and was gravity-fed into the petrol tank of your vehicle. A Mr. Ernest Bates owned the cottage at this time. The land to the right-hand side of the picture has been developed and now contains houses and car sales businesses.

4   This was Derby Road from the top of Oat Hill at the turn of the twentieth century. The grassy fields on either side of the road belonged to the farm in the centre of the picture. A handoperated water pump and a gritstone trough were on the opposite side of the road to the farm. The gasworks was built in 1838 and housed two horizontal retorts and one-and-a-half gasometers. The streets were gaslit at this time. The church tower and Barrel Edge can be seen in the distance. This was the southerly limit of development of the town at this time.

5   The view from Derby Road looking towards Canterbury Terrace with the church tower in the centre background and Barrel Edge on the upper right.

The cottage in the centre of the picture on Water Lane was derelict around 1950 and pulled down a few years later. The field in the foreground now contains a clothing factory that has only recently closed. A modern housing estate has also been built on part of the field in the last few years.

WIRKSWORTH FROM THE SOUTH.

6   On the extreme left was the gasworks with the gas manager's house next door. On the right side of the picture Harold Wayne, joiner and builder, owned a large wooden building at this time. The last owner was Mr. Buxton and during the 1950s it was used for garaging cars at 25p per week. The gasworks and wooden building were demolished to allow road improvements to the junctions of Summer Lane and Water Lane in the 1960s. Buildings were also present in front of the Wheatsheaf public house. The remains of a doorway and window can be seen in the wall below the Wheatsheaf.

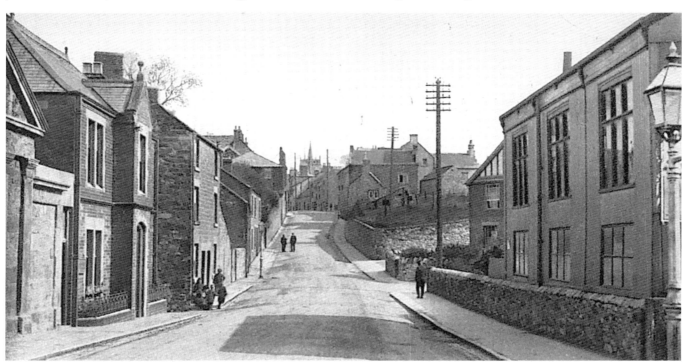

7 Looking westwards over the Meadows in the early years of the twentieth century, with only Meadow House and Yokecliffe Farm occupying the landscape. The limekiln to the left of Meadow House was last thought to have been used in 1860. The land to the right of Meadow House and above Yokecliffe Lane was used for garden allotments. The fields are now covered with a modern housing estate, which was built from around 1960 to the present date. The farm was demolished in 1986.

8 Looking eastwards along Yokecliffe around 1905. Beneath the steeply wooded slope of Yokecliffe was a lead vein called the Yokecliffe Rake that ran from Wirksworth to Brassington. This vein was a prolific producer of lead and there are numerous old mineshafts in this area, some of which were worked from the seventeenth century onwards. The largest mine was the Yokecliffe Mine, whose capped shaft is still clearly visible, but there were others smaller mines like Boams, Primrose, Rooses, Jack I' Th' Ash and Bayards Bank. The mineral tips in the centre of the picture were re-worked in these early years for lead, caulk (barytes) and fluorspar.

9 The view from the top of Yokecliffe from a postcard published by A. Barker, who had a printing works in West End. The road in the left foreground is Yokecliffe Lane. Gilkin and Breamfield are on the extreme left, the hamlet of Gorsey Bank on the right and the Meadows and Water Lane are in the centre of the picture. Today most of the fields to the centre and right of the picture are full of houses and factories, built since the First World War. The town's windmill stood here-abouts.

10   In the space opposite the Wheatsheaf Inn was the site of a well-dressing. Well-dressings were called tap-dressings in Wirksworth and the custom was started in 1827 to thank a number of local gentry who clubbed together and had water brought down from the Moor in wooden pipes to taps in seven parts of the town. The festival day was the Wednesday of Whit week and this dressing dates from before the First World War. At this time, the picture in the centre panel often depicted water, since there were still water shortages in the Wirksworth area. Wars, churches and local scenes were also used in the centre panels. Religious panels did not appear until just before the Second World War. This scene portrays Groudle Glen in the Isle of Man.

11   Around 1905, James Watterson assembled the local children and the drovers to pose for this photograph. St John Street used to be known as Nether Street. Nether House is on the right and the stables were to the right of the horse and cart. This was home of the Toplis family and later the town house of the Hurt family. In 1930 the house was owned by the Chadwick family and used as a guesthouse. The house was pulled down in 1937 and the cinema and country club were erected in the space. Some of the houses on both sides of the street have not changed in the last hundred years.

12 The demolition of Nether House in 1938. The men on the roof were removing the chimney pots. The shop on the left was Slater's wireless shop and the signs were advertising Marconiphone. Mr. Slater was also one of the local coal merchants. He served for many years on the local council and was known as the 'Father of Wirksworth's Council'. The shop became one of Wirksworth institutions selling radios, cigarettes, tobacco, sweets, batteries, bulbs etc. The interior of the shop never changed, but sadly closed in the mid-1980s with the death of Mrs. Slater.

13   The cinema was a popular entertainment after the Second World War and was, with a seating capacity of 500, large for the size of the town. The shop on the left of the cinema was a confectionery/café and the one on the right was a florist and green grocery. The woman kneeling in the front of the shop was Mrs. E. Webster. The cinema program changed every two days and seat prices at this time were circle 11p (2/3d) and stalls 7,5p (1/6d). There were two performances per evening at around 5 and 7.45 p.m. and two films were shown at each performance. A matinee for children was held on Saturday afternoon and cost 2.5 pence. Before the days of television, the film industry provided a varied program of entertainment in contrast to the cinema of today. The cinema closed in 1967 and is now a builder's merchant.

14 On the west side of St. John Street was Waltham House, the home of George Hanson Wheatcroft. He owned Haarlem and Speedwell Mills. The house was purchased for £1,000, together with the adjacent cottage for £350, in 1927 for use as a Cottage Hospital. This hospital was to replace the existing hospital – Babington House on Greenhill. A further £800 was needed to fit out the hospital making a total of £2,150. £1,972 had been raised from legacies and donations and this left a deficit of nearly £200. A carnival was held during Wakes week in September 1927 to raise in excess of this sum. The local community funded hospitals at this time.

15 A photograph taken soon after the opening of the hospital in 1928 showing the architecture at the rear of the building. Considerable alterations were carried out when the maternity hospital was converted to the present medical centre. The right-hand bay windows and building have been demolished to make an entrance to the car park, which has now covered the old gardens.

16 Staff and patients of Wirksworth Cottage Hospital in 1928 or 1929. Back row: Mrs. Millward, Agnes Lowe, Matron Norris, a private nurse and nurse Green. The little girl is Francis Ford. Front row: Fanny Green, Mr. Wint (Brassington) and a private nurse.

17   Sarah, Elizabeth and John Slater standing in the doorway of the shop at number 1 St. Mary's Gate in the early years of the last century. Around 1950, this was a toy shop selling Meccano and Hornby trains and was run by Mr. and Mrs. Millward. Later the shop was a haberdashery, a green grocery and is now an Italian restaurant. At this time, Webster's lorry depot, whose vehicles had a green and yellow livery, was further along St. Mary's Gate.

18   The baker's shop on St. Mary's Gate which had recently been taken over by Luke Hall of Steeplegrange from Fred Baggaley at the turn of the twentieth century. This shop was established in 1844 and has been a bakery for the past hundred years. The bakery still uses traditional coke ovens, which are housed in a very old building at the rear of the shop.

19 Around 1900 Frederick Brailsford, who was a barber and also made umbrellas, ran the shop on the right. This shop had a barber's business for over ninety years. The building in the centre with a balcony and a large sign was a shop with a Temperance Hotel above. On the left the present Lloyds TSB Bank was Moore and Robinsons Bank and the manager at this time was Henry Beesley. The bank was amalgamated with the Capitol and Counties Bank in April 1901. Toplis, who had a tannery and other business interests in the town, originally started the bank in 1780. The bank became a partnership between Toplis and Richard Arkwright in 1800.

20   This scene shows St. John Street in the 1920s. Horse and carts were still the main form of transport. The shop on the right was an ironmonger's, next door was a butcher's shop run by James Frith, then Burgons the grocer's and tea dealer's with the Temperance Hotel sign plainly visible above the shop. To the left of the cart in the centre of the picture was a woman in a wheel chair in the shop doorway of J. Rains, butcher. Two doors to the left of this shop, with the barber's pole above the door, was another hairdresser's.

21 A similar scene to the last one taken thirty years later. The shops from left to right were: Woodford (men's hairdresser) private house, J. Rains and Sons (butcher's), women's clothes shop, Burgons (groceries and provision) ladies' hairdressing salon Watts, (private house), Watts, (photographer's) Corner House with radios and radiograms in the window and Maskrey's, (cigarette and sweet shop).

22 A timeless scene in the early years of the 1900s taken by a local photographer – James Watterson. There was a shop in the far end of the Hope and Anchor that sold fish and game and was run by William Wheatcroft. The entrance to the Hope and Anchor is plain with steps and railings. Every window had a box of flowers. The shop on the left was a pharmacy run by James Hindle. Apart from some minor alterations very little has changed architecturally in the last hundred years.

J. Watterson, Photo.,   St. John Street, Wirksworth.   A. Barker & Sons, Printers.

23 A view inside the chemist's shop with all the medicines neatly arranged in bottles on the shelves. Only the front portion of the shop was used for the pharmacy and the shop was only enlarged in progressive stages after the Second World War. The glass-fronted displays on the counter contained ointments and pills and a chair was provided for the convenience of customers. The placard on the counter was advertising Bismuthated Magnesia for aiding digestion. The man in the photograph has not been identified.

24 The archway on the left was part of the Crown Inn, which was first mentioned in 1758 and closed around 1910. It was an old coaching inn. Bradley's, the men's outfitter's, continued to trade to around 1970. The corner buildings were Marsdens, churn and bath maker, general and agricultural ironmonger. Mr. Symonds, one of the town's solicitors, occupied the house with 14 windows on the right and this building dates from the middle of the eighteenth century. On the extreme right was one of the shops demolished for the building of Harrison Drive.

25 Prior to 1938, there was a row of shops on the present-day Market Place which was demolished when Harrison Drive was built. The shop on the left was a tobacconist, next door was Thomas Millington, a watchmaker and jeweller. The next large shop was the Wirksworth and District Co-operative Society, which moved to the position of the present Ken's Minimarket near the Dale in 1910-1911. Hiltons shoe shop and Hunter's tea stores were on the right side of the road. Beneath the window on the right are some wooden dolly pegs, which were common washday accessories until the introduction of the electrical washing machine in the 1950s.

Market Place, Wirksworth.

26   Examples of two of the tap-dressings which stood in West End. The one on the left was dressed in 1902 and showed Conway Castle and Telford's Bridge. The shells in the sky probably related to the Boer War. The tap-dressing on the right was dated 1906 and showed an unknown church. The top panels show the insignia for Edwardus Rex and Georgius Rex.

27   A scene taken between 1920 and 1930. On the immediate left was Hunter's Tea Stores. The present NatWest Bank was previously the Crompton and Evans' Union Bank and next door was Johnson's, the ironmonger's, with various goods displayed on the pavement. The building to the left again used to be the Greyhound Inn, which was first mentioned in 1827, closed around 1913 and was a shop at this moment in time. An early motorcycle was in front of this shop. A solitary gaslamp illuminated the Market Place.

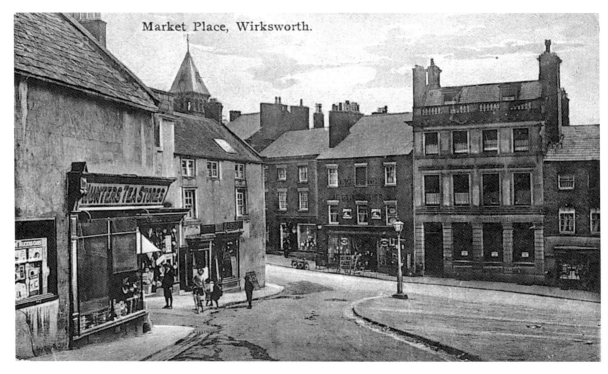

Market Place, Wirksworth.

28 Harrison Drive was built in 1938 to 1940 to relieve the traffic problems in the heavily congested Coldwell Street and North End since these were main roads through the town. Before Harrison Drive was constructed, there were two houses in the position of the road. The building next to the Red Lion was Watts, wireless dealer and taxi proprietor and adjacent was Doxey's, newsagent and tearooms. The building of this road required the movement of the Market Place to its present position. The small opening near the corner of Marsden's was the entrance to the extensive cellars beneath the shop.

29   Marsden's around 1950 with a varied display of tools and agricultural implements for sale in front of the shop. In the early 1900s, Marsdens won many awards for the quality of their milk churns and Sitz baths. The local farmers used milk churns to send their milk by cart and rail to the creameries. The Sitz baths were used in the hydros in Matlock for the tepid water cure and Marsdens had an office in Smedley Street, Matlock near to the hydros. Marsdens employed some very good tradesmen. The price of goods in the shop was coded and was marked in letters of the alphabet on each item. The business closed in 1982 after trading in Wirksworth since 1764. The shops to the right of Marsdens were the newsagent, Hawley's the pork butcher's and Coates the butcher's.

WKH. 12   The Market Place, Wirksworth.

30 A large gathering in the old Market Place. It was most likely a Sunday School celebration as two of the banners read Wirksworth Congregational Sunday School and the Baptist Sunday School. The photograph was taken by W. Winter of Derby. The date is unknown but was most likely Edwardian judging by the long dresses and straw boaters. S. Ogden's butcher's shop is on the centre left of the picture with William Fox's shop next door. On the right were the two shops prior to the building of Harrison Drive.

31   A photograph of William Fox's shop by James Watterson. He was a general draper, hosier and glover. He sold I & R Morley's superior hosiery, Dent's renowned gloves, linoleum, oilcloths, mattings, mats and thoroughly shrunk wool flannels were a specialty. Funerals were also furnished. Large gaslamps hung in front of the shop windows. This shop is now occupied by the present-day Ken's Top Mini Market.

32 At the entrance to the Dale were two wine and spirit shops run by Mainprice and Company. One of the shops was in Dale House (left side). The other shop on the right jutted a fair way into the road and this building had been restored in the 1980s to a completely different design. Pictures of the Dale and Greenhill were few and this must have been a rare event with the adults and children posing for the photographer.

33 One of the oldest houses in Wirksworth is Babington House on Greenhill, which was built for a wealthy merchant about 1630. An unusual feature is the sundial on the right gable. From 1724 to 1829 it was used as a workhouse and became a Cottage Hospital from 1867 to 1927. There were eleven beds – three for casualty and eight for illness. Casualties were taken in via steps at the rear of the building. Quarry men paid 2d (1p) per week to Cottage Hospital funds. The woman in the white cap and apron is probably nurse Penny. The house is now a private residence.

34 There were two public houses in the Dale – The Recruiting Sergeant and the William the Fourth. Every year there was a tap-dressing in the Dale near the William the Fourth. The tap-dressing on the left won third prize and had a small fountain in the fore-ground. The scene depicts a stream running through a valley. The scene on the right tap-dressing depicts Florence Nightingale. Both were dressed some time between 1902 and 1940 and both remind people of the gift of water in the text.

35 The date – the 2nd of March 1933. The thaw has started and the snow is starting to melt. There was plenty of snow that winter, which brought severe difficulties to the town. Surrounding villages could be cut off for weeks. No gritters in those days – only horse-drawn snowploughs and shovels. Wirksworth Town Council also had a small horse-drawn snowplough specially for clearing the pavements. Watts wireless shop is on the left of the Red Lion Hotel and has a radio aerial on the front of the building. This area was also the terminus for the local bus services.

36   In this 1950s scene, the shops from right to left were Hunters (grocers), S. J. Livingstone (men's outfitter), London Central Meat Company (butchers), Hilton's shoe shop, Spencer's fish and chip shop and Atkinsons (high class grocers). The notice boards on the left side of the Red Lion Hotel were the bus timetables for the North Western Road Car Company and the Trent Motor Traction Company. North Western operated the route Wirksworth to Matlock and Trent Wirksworth to Derby. All the buildings at this time had their original stone or brick frontages.

37 A view down Coldwell Street in 1905 showing the two houses attached to the Red Lion Hotel. The building jutting into the street below the Town Hall was that of James Watterson's music shop. He was also a local photographer. Previously the following buildings stood on the Town Hall site: King's Head and Spread Eagle public houses, a dwelling house and shop occupied by Mr. Palin and a dwelling house occupied by Mr. Baxter. The buildings were purchased for £1,500 and were demolished in 1871. The Town Hall was built in a Gothic style at a cost of £5,800 and was opened in 1873.

The Town Council purchased the building on 21 November 1901. The present-day Rates Office was a butcher's shop at the turn of the twentieth century.

38 This scene of around 1950 shows the War Memorial beneath the footbridge. This Memorial has been moved in the last few years to a more prominent position opposite the Memorial Hall in St. John Street. Both sides of the road had rows of Rowan trees and the old Baileycroft Quarry to the left of the road was used as the local tip for household and general waste. The building on the far left is the Junior School and at this time Mr. G. Guise was the headmaster. The area to the right of the road was Wirksworth Council's Highway Depot.

BOLEHILL, WIRKSWORTH.

39 Looking towards the town centre from the Red Lion Hotel around 1910, showing some of the buildings which existed prior to the present Market Place. There was a shop to the right of the Hope and Anchor and a narrow road led down to the Causeway. The building behind the horse and cart was a chemist's shop. To the right of Marsdens was a china shop (present-day newsagents) and next door was a tailor's shop run by S. Land. On the left-hand side we have Atkinsons, high-class grocers, and next door large gaslamps were present in front of the windows beneath the sunblinds. On the next building the sign of the Greyhound Inn is just visible.

40   The Red Lion Hotel is an eighteenth-century coaching and posting inn and at the time of this picture Amos Brentnall was the proprietor. The hotel was a stop on the turnpike that connected Alfreton with Ashbourne. The hotel boasted a motor garage, good stabling and a bowling green. The fourth building on the right was the wine and spirit shop of Charles Wright. This was a large business with offices in Leith and London. The Vaults public house and the wine and spirit stores were round the corner on the site of the present Barmote Croft car park. The vehicle on the left was one of the first vans in Wirksworth and most probably belonged to Watts, the wireless dealer, whose shop is behind the van.

41 Inside Charles Wright's malt whisky bottling department that was in buildings, which used to stand on the site of the Barmoot Croft car park. This was one of the large staple businesses in the town. Glen Haddon and Old Gran were whisky trade marks of Charles Wright. Glen Haddon was a seven-year-old whisky and Old Gran was ten years old. The business was mentioned in 1797 and continued until 1962. Charles Wright, who died on 5th June 1912, was one of the town's prominent businessmen. He supported many of the town's institutions, especially the cricket club.

42 The churchyard with white gravestones lying in a chequered pattern. Numerous trees and shrubs were present in the early years of the last century and gave the churchyard a more rural atmosphere, in contrast to the stark scene of today. On the left somewhere beneath the beech tree is the unmarked grave of Elizabeth Evans, a staunch Methodist preacher on whom the character Dinah Morris in George Eliot's 'Adam Bede' was based. The vicarage on the right was built in 1806 in the Regency style. The graveyard was last used around 1860.

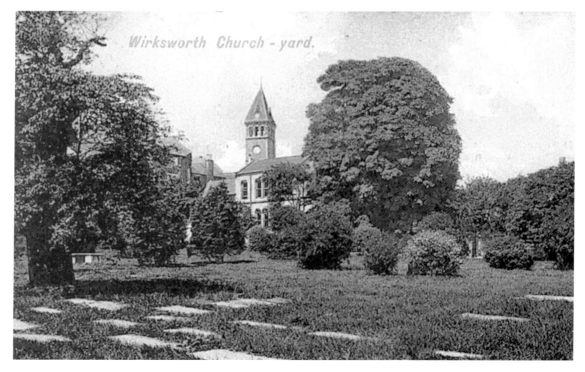

Wirksworth Church - yard.

43 The roof over the nave was raised in Sir George Gilbert Scott's restoration of 1876. Prior to restoration there were castellations at the tops of the walls of the nave, chancel, north and south transepts and these were removed except for those on the west end. The upper windows in the north transept were removed when the new roof was added. The west front was also restored in 1907 with a new west door. A new lower roof was added to the nave in 1926, due to the poor state of the Yorkshire grey states.

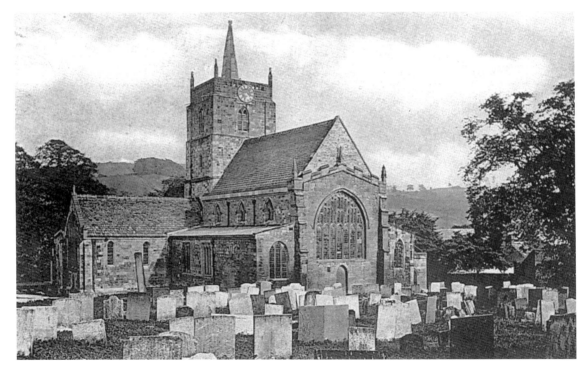

44   One of the most recent changes in the church was the removal of the organ, which had become uneconomic to repair. A modern, electronic equivalent was purchased and stands between the left pair of pillars beneath the tower. A refectory has now been built in the vacated organ space. The chandeliers were found discarded outside the church during the Second World War and most likely went for scrap.

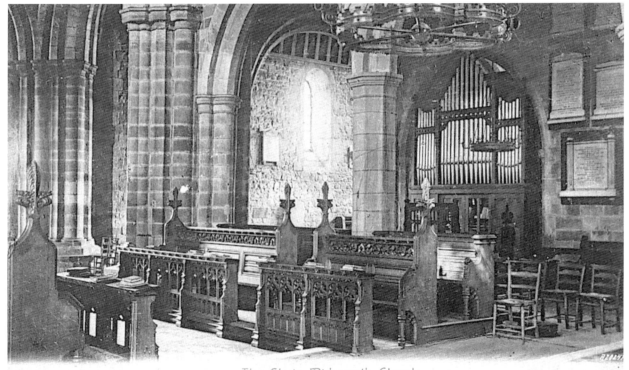

The Choir, Wirksworth Church.

45 An unusual postcard postmarked 18/8/1906 showing a ceremony of which nothing is known. The photograph was taken in the vicarage garden with the church in the background. Each girl held flowers and represented a county. 39 English and Welsh counties were represented.

46 Looking towards the north-west of the town from the top of the church tower. The vicarage is in the front right foreground with the Methodist Chapel and Charles Wright's premises behind. The Town Hall is on the left with part of the Dale behind. The Baileycroft and Middlepeak Quarries have engulfed the fields in the background and this area of hillside no longer exists.

View from Church Tower (North West), Wirksworth.

47 Looking towards the north-east of the town from the top of the church tower. In the lower centre of the picture is the old grammar school. The house on the lower left has been demolished together with some of the buildings behind the school. Above these buildings can be seen the tower on the National School on North End. On the right below the New-bridge School was the bell tower on top of the old stables to Wirksworth Hall. This part of the stables was demolished in 1968 to widen the section of Cold-well Street before the railway bridge.

View from Church Tower (North East), Wirksworth.

48 The trees on the left have gone. Anthony Gell of Hopton Hall founded the school in 1576. The school in the picture was built in 1828 at a cost of £1,664 and was designed by a local builder – John Maskrey. It was used until 1908 as a school and then used as an annex for teaching woodwork and domestic science until the comprehensive school was built in 1965. The building has been converted to a residence and to manufacture reproduction furniture. Anthony Gell also founded the almshouses around 1584 to house six poor men.

49 The old priest's house as seen from the Hannages dates from the sixteenth century. This was one of the oldest priest's houses in the country and one of the oldest buildings in Wirksworth. In the early 1950's, the roof had collapsed and it was demolished a few years later due to the dangerous condition. The steps to the building are still to be seen from Blind Lane but the rest of the building remains as a pile of rubble. After the Second World War there was no money for the restoration of old buildings.

CHURCH AND OLD PRIEST'S HOUSE, WIRKSWORTH.   5095.

50 The rear of Wirksworth Hall as photographed by E. L. Scrivens around 1920. The rear of the postcard states 'the big Hall has all fell in. It was built over an old mine'.

The house was rebuilt in 1779 for Charles Hurt and his wife Susannah, who was the daughter of Sir Richard Arkwright. The architect for the rebuilding was almost certainly Joseph Pickford of Derby. The hall was two-and-a-half storeys in height and the picture shows the two bay single-storey ballroom which was added in the nineteenth century. The house was sold in 1858 to Nicholas Wood and to a local person in 1918. The house was demolished in 1922.

E.L.S.245-6. The Hall And Church, Wirksworth.

51 The station around 1890 was busy with the movement of people, animals and milk from the local farms and limestone and lime from the quarries. The animal pens were immediately behind the station and the station house, good's shed and Cemetery Lane bridge can be seen in the distance. The wagons on the left were labelled the Wirksworth Stone and Mineral Company and carried stone from Baileycroft Quarry. A number of milk churns are on the platform. Signal levers can also be seen near the opening in the fence. In 1865 cottages were pulled down for the building of the station which was completed in 1867.

52 Another photograph by James Watterson taken in 1906 showing an auto-train consisting of a Midland and Great Northern Railway 4-4-0T No. 10 and an ex-Midland Railway Pullman Car No. 5, which was originally named Minerva. The train ran between Wirksworth, Melbourne and Ripley until 1911. The signal box is visible to the left of the train.

53 A view taken in 1938 by F. W. Scarratt of Derby showing the railway lines in front of the station full of wagons. The Wirksworth Quarry wagons would travel up the tunnel beneath Wirksworth to the 'Big Hole' (Dale) quarry using a Hudswell Clarke No. 1611 0-4-0 saddle tank shunter. The quantity of minerals passing through Wirksworth Station was in excess of 100,00 tons per year at this period of time. The small building to the left was the weighbridge and the houses above the station are those on North End. All the station buildings on the Wirksworth to Duffield branch were built to the same design.

54 These two tap-dressings were situated on North End near Beech House. The frames were of differing design. The dressing on the left won second prize in 1914 and shows a couple crossing the river via a small footbridge. Grazing cattle and a building are in the background. The dressing on the right depicts Adam Bede's Cottage on Derby Road. Both dressings mention water in the text.

Wirksworth Well Dressing, Second Prize, 1914

55 The Moot Hall houses the Barmote Court, which still meets to settle any lead mining matters in the Low Peak. The court is one of the oldest industrial courts in the land. In 1773, a Moot Hall was built in front of the Red Lion on the north side of the Market Place. Due to the rowdy behaviour and congestion by the miners, this building was demolished and the hall on this picture built in Chapel Lane in 1814. The two bas-relief plaques showing the miner's tools were removed from the old hall and reset in the façade of this building.

Moot Hall, Wirksworth.

56   A view of Bolehill prior to 1920. There were only a few houses on the road upto Steeplegrange and only one house on New Road at this time. Bolehill was an old lead-mining settlement and the spoil heap of Bage Mine is clearly visible. In the centre were wagons in the loading dock area, where lime and limestone brought down from Stoneycroft and Middle Peak Quarries were tipped into the wagons. The sidings were fed by two tramways. Another line to Stoneycroft Quarry passed through the gates on the lower right of the picture.

57 This picture shows Holwell No. 3 0-4-0T celebrating its centenary, having been built in 1873 by Black Hawthorn at Gateshead. This locomotive together with another by the name of Uppingham transported huge quantities of limestone from the lower levels of Stoneycroft Quarry passing under Middleton Road to the loading docks on Cromford Road. This locomotive is now with a preservation society. Behind the locomotive is a large pile of limestone for the sugar beet processing plants in Lincolnshire.

58 Looking eastwards down Stoneycroft Quarry around 1920 with the sidings running to the quarry faces. Mr. John Shaw, who began burning lime on the west side of Middleton Road, started the quarry in 1830. Lime has always been produced in this quarry, together with enormous amounts of limestone for the steelworks at Corby. The limestone, after blasting, was broken to the required size manually with a sixteen pound hammer, locally known as a 'maw'. If smaller stone was needed a knapping hammer was used.

59 There were numerous lime kilns in the lower quarries on Middleton Road. After the Second World War, lime was produced in Stoneycroft Quarry in a coke-fired kiln, which used to belch thick black smoke when it was fired up. The lime was transported by rail to the loading dock on Cromford Road in sealed or covered wagons using the shunters. In later years a gas-fired kiln was used and lime was transported to the loading dock in the station by lorries. The quarry was restored in 1993 with the aid of a land restoration grant.

60   Another view looking towards Bolehill and Barrel Edge prior to 1920. The tramway running into the picture from the left carried narrow gauge wagons to transport limestone from Middle Peak Quarry to the loading dock on Cromford Road. A small diesel locomotive was used to shunt the wagons from the quarry face to the top of the incline in the 1940s. The tramway was replaced by an overhead conveyor when Middle Peak Quarry was mechanized in the mid-1950's. Beneath the field in the foreground was the site of the Twentylands lead mine. The spoil heaps to the George Mine are on the right above the house.

61 A rare view looking from the west side of the Monkey Hole Quarry towards Black Rocks. The quarry had a branch line that ran across Middleton Road and through Middleton Wharf to the Cromford and High Peak Railway line. The bridge connected Rise End at Middleton with the houses at the top of Greenhill and the Dale. In the 1950's and 1960's, the quarry was used by the Electricity Companies for testing the stability of electricity pylons. Forces were applied to the pylon via ropes and pulleys attached to the rock face to simulate adverse weather conditions.

62 The Cromford and High Peak Railway was important to the local economy, transporting limestone from the local quarries to the Midland main line at High Peak Junction. On the left was the siding to Middleton Wharf, upper Middle Peak and Monkey Hole Quarries. A wagon loaded with limestone is descending the Middleton Incline, which had a gradient of 1 in 8.25. In the foreground is a water tanker waiting to ascend. Tankers were used to provide water to settlements along the line. The chains on the right-hand buffer were used to plait the wagon to the wire rope.

63 Middleton Top Engine House is now a landmark on the horizon but it used to be partly hidden behind a hill, which has been quarried away over the last forty years. This view inside the engine room was dated 23/4/1913 and shows the 14-foot diameter cast-iron driving wheel on the right-hand side. On the left is one of the cylinders that operated on a steam pressure of 5 p.s.i. The winding engine was built in 1825 by the Butterley Iron Works and worked continuously until the incline closed on 12th August 1963. The names of the two men are not known.

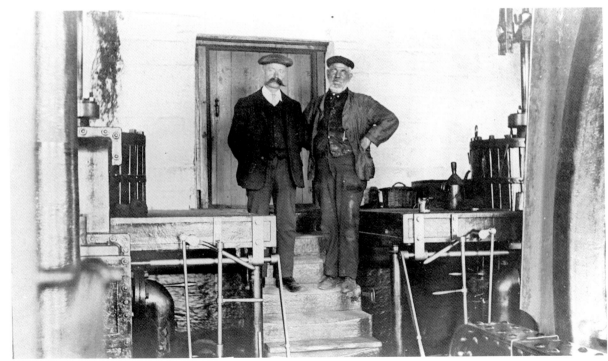

64 Looking south over Wirksworth in this photograph by James Watterson of around 1905. To the right of Cromford Road was the loading dock where limestone from the quarries was tipped into main line wagons. The sidings in Wirksworth Station can be seen on the left. The engine house to the Meerbrook Sough Mine together with the beehives over the Meerbrook Sough can be seen to the left of Cromford Road. Stoneycroft Quarry is on the immediate right and Baileycroft Quarry is just visible in front of the Town Hall and church towers.

65   Steeplegrange as seen in 1926 by F. W. Scarratt of Derby showing the photographer's bull nose Morris Cowley in the centre of the picture. The house next to the bridge was built by Arkwright and was the Railway Inn in the nineteenth century, but has been a farmhouse for many years. The bridge carried the Cromford and High Peak Railway. The house on the right, Rose Cottage, was advertising mineral waters and afternoon teas. At the end of the Victorian age, the cottage was advertising apartments to let. A beautiful wrought iron greenhouse used to exist on the right-hand side of the cottage but today a two-storey extension has been added in its place.

66 A view of Bolehill. The name Bolehill means the site of a bole, which was a furnace for smelting lead. Bolehill was a mining community and industry revolved around mining in the Bage, George and Hallam lead mines. The Bage Mine produced 2,245 tons of lead between 1872 and 1887 and worked between 1868 and 1908. The Bage mine was also the source of two rare minerals – Matlockite and Cromfordite. Near to the house on the right is the Hallam shaft that connects with the Meerbrook Sough. This was one of the last soughs to be driven in Derbyshire. It was started in 1772 and by 1846 had cost £70,000. It drains the Wirksworth and Middleton areas and with all its branches has a total length of 5 miles. Francis Hurt was a principal of the sough proprietors.

67 Looking from Oaker-thorpe Road westwards towards Cromford Road. Some of the houses we see on Cromford Road today have not yet been built in this postcard of around 1904. The spoil heaps to the Meerbrook (middle right) and Twentylands mines (upper right) were clearly visible. Baileycroft quarry was on the left and the wall above the quarry is the position of the present-day footpath be-tween Greenhill and Middleton Road. The smoke was from the large number of limekilns in the Stoneycroft and Middle Peak Quarries. The two tramways from the quar-ries are clearly visible.

68   A view of Wirksworth from Gilkin one hundred years ago. In the centre of the picture were Wirksworth Hall and gardens with the stables on both sides of Coldwell Street. On the right was the station and above this, the road leads to Middleton. Dale Quarry (Big Hole) between the Dale and Greenhill was small and insignificant. Baileycroft, Stoneycroft and Middle Peak Quarries are on the right. Green fields were present between Greenhill and Middleton Road. The Hannages is the field in the centre left of the picture with the railway in the foreground. The picture illustrates how much land around the town has been quarried away in the last century.

69 Long distance views are valuable for recording changes. This scene was taken in the late 1920's and in the lower right, Wirksworth Hall has gone but the gardens still remain. There was a lot of dust rising from Dale Quarry and the quarry is much larger. A stone crusher was installed in this quarry in 1925-1926 and the noise and dust from the machinery made living near the quarry unbearable. The houses around the quarry were covered in a layer of limestone dust, which penetrated every nook and cranny. Nether House and gardens can be seen to the left of the picture.

70   In the early 1950s, there was a big change in the quarrying industry in Wirksworth – mechanization. In the picture to the right of Middle Peak quarry can be seen the overhead conveyor under construction, which would bring limestone from the quarry to the newly-constructed hoppers at the Cromford Road sidings. At this time, this modernization was to give Wirksworth the second largest quarrying plant in Europe. This plant only required 25 men for operation, so all the other quarrymen (approximately 500) were made redundant and had to find work in the surrounding areas.

WIRKSWORTH FROM GILKILN.

71 Gilkin used to be topped with trees, which were cut down by the farmer around 1925. The two men ploughing the steep field to the south of Gilkin and adjacent to the wood next to St. Helen's Lane were Sam and Ben Beardsley. When tractors became common in the 1930s, 25 percent of the land went out of arable use because tractors could not cope with steep sloping fields.

Gilkin Hill.

72 A view of the southern part of the town from St. Helen's Lane circa 1950, with Gorsey Bank in the left foreground. The grammar school is on the centre right and above can be seen the clouds of dust rising from the quarries which used to cover the town when the wind was in the right direction. Wooded Yokecliffe is near the top of the picture. The green fields between Water Lane, Derby Road, Arkwright Street and most of the Meadows have now been built on to provide houses and factories as the town has grown in size.

General View of Wirksworth.   3.

73 The hamlet of Gorsey Bank has changed very little in the past hundred years. In the foreground is Providence Mill, built around 1885 and was surrounded by houses.

In 1890 the mill was powered by a gas engine, which was probably fed from the local gasworks in Warmbrook.

A sawmill mentioned in 1823 was previously on this site. To the left of the picture was a wooded area, some of which was cut down when the council houses were built in 1926-1927. On the left was a shop that is obscured by a tree in this picture. At this time W. Brooks ran the shop and this valuable store continued trading upto 1978.

74 Looking towards the town centre from Gorsey Bank around 1940. On the right-hand side is Willowbath Mill with the railway running across the centre of the picture. The grammar school can be seen above the mill. In the centre of the picture are the houses at the top of Bournebrook Avenue and Willowbath Lane with Arkwright Street in the distance. Today the area above the railway has been developed to provide houses and factories. The land in front of the railway line was used as a refuse tip but was landscaped to form a recreation ground for the residents of Gorsey Bank.

75 This view from the top of the railway cutting between the chestnut trees shows the grammar school and the picture dates to around 1950. The tennis courts are in front of the school. This part of the school was built between the two world wars. To the left of the school are the Wheatsheaf Inn and the Army Cadet building. In the far distance Middle Peak has not been quarried away. The land to the left below the school was used as garden allotments.

WIRKSWORTH

76 This part of the grammar school was built in 1908 to replace the one in the churchyard and now forms the present-day Gell block. The footpath running from the left to the centre was a convenient access for residents of the Derby Road and Gorsey Bank housing estates to the shops in the town. The modern comprehensive school that was built in 1965 now covers this area.

GRAMMAR SCHOOL, WIRKSWORTH.